# The Paranormal Magazine

# Volume Four

# LIKE US!
## ON FACEBOOK

### www.facebook.com/theparanormalmagazine

---

Our New WEBSITE
http://paranormal-magazine.com

---

### <u>WIN A Signed Copy Of Issue 5</u>
Give an honest REVIEW of our book to win a signed copy of issue 5

Please visit amazon.co.uk or .com to write the review about this book.

# Lee Steer
Author – Editor

# Wayne Ridsdel
Illustrator, Author

# Co Authors
Philip Willaims
John Williams

The Paranormal magazine

A Unique ghost hunting magazine.
Brought to you from the 2 minds of: Lee Steer, Wayne Ridsdel,
With help from Philip & john William and friends of our series.

The mission is to Educate, and showcase the world of the paranormal.
Featuring Famous Haunting's, Paranormal A to Z, Ghost Hunting
Equipment's, How to Makes, Myths and legends,
Ghost Pictures BUSTED, Old traditions, Ghost Pictures,
New Hauntings, and much more..

Thanks for showing an interest in our official paranormal magazine
series
All enquires please email
Asteer8@aol.com

# Contents

## A to z

K, L, n

-

EXORCISM

▪

The Amazing Saga of Florence Cook and
Katie King

▪

RIP

▪

conducting an EVP session

▪

Ghost hunters by Jeff

▪

drakelow tunnels shadow factory

▪

My home, The Cage St Osyth

▪

wiccan foods

▪

Vernal Equinox, 20th March 2014

▪

# Interview

## Alexandra Holzer

■

## Ghost Gallery

■

## Lifting  spirits

■

## Devils  toy box

■

## atdd teddy

■

## issue 5

■

## Ghost Hunts

## A to Z

In each issue we cover 3 letters from the a to z.
This issue we will cover
G, H, I

# **J**ersey Devil

A mythical Creature, which has had more then 2000+ sightings in the
New Jersey Pinelands, a legend so serious, it made Schools and
factories close down.

For 260 years the myth definitely terrorized the towns of new Jersey,
At 2:30 am, a Mr. & Mrs. Nelson Evans described the jersey devil
having a dog like head, "collie" three feet tall,  having a long neck, and
small scale dragon like wings, and horse like hooves, with long
straight legs which it stands up on like a bird.

This creature has been known to bark like a dog,  and has been seen
flying away.

The above picture is a detailed sketch of the sightings, some people describe the creature looking different, but all have similar characteristics, Could this be a mutated dog, or is this something much more sinister which we don't understand?

Picture by http://ghost2ghost.org/jersey-devil/

# **K**arma

Karma is known as a unknown supernatural Power, which came from the Hindu and Buddhist religions,   Karma means if you do something bad, karma will come back and bite you, Meaning Something bad will happen to you in return, It is the same things as doing something good, karma may come back and reward you.

Some examples are,
You Steal from a good friend = someone close to you will steal from you.
You give some money to an homeless man = You will win a lottery ticket prize
Do you see karma as supernatural? Please leave us your comments.

# Leylines

ley lines they are to some people mystical lines of magical power, lines of earth's natural energy, walkways of the ancients or just don't exist. Either way there are many books, articles and theories about them. It's not just the new age spiritualists and alternate dimensional people that believe or study them. This subject has captured the minds of some of the greatest thinkers of our species, Newton and Tesla been two of them.

When it comes to Tesla he believed in a energy grid of the planet. Yes this was a grid of natural energy that could be captured and used by us as a clean energy. Lets say this is correct then maybe the ancients picked up on this and followed these lines of energy to survive. They say flowing water is energy, lines of limestone, animals following certain paths to survive.

Lets say the lines of certain materials within the ground create a lower resistance acting then as a conductor for the earths energy.
My first personnel thought to this after studying acupressure was this could be compared to the acupressure points of the body. Its the same principle, the body has been found to have fibrous tissue with a low resistance and these act as paths for our body to conduct energy from certain points (this also explains chackra points). Already we are covering so many ideas it could be easy to get lost in confusion, i will make some quick bullet points of what i have found.

- Ley lines are the alignment of megaliths, monuments and places of particular interest. Some say these lines are manmade lines of power using stones rocks and other objects to direct power or amplify.
- Curry lines are lines of the earth's natural radiation; some say detectable with dowsing rods and picking the right spot and living in the right line of radiation could be beneficial for one's life. Like all things in nature the wrong spot can be harmful.
- Black lines have been described has a depressive negative energy. These can be in buildings as a mist or fog or line.
- Hartmann lines these been more complicated. These are more magnetic in nature with a grid over the planet. The zones in between these lines that push up from the earth's surface are localized environments. These environments are said to be delicate to the seasons and hours of the day.

Written by john Williams

# Redridge co owner

# EXORCISM

## BY Wayne Ridsdel

Exorcism comes from the Greek word *Exorkismos'* meaning *'binding by oath';* it is a ritual practiced to evict demons or other spiritual entities from a person or location that are believed to be possessed. The procedure varies greatly depending on the spiritual beliefs of the exorcist, but is usually done by causing the entity to swear an oath, carrying out an elaborate ritual, or simply by commanding it to depart in the name of a higher divine power. The practice of exorcism is an ancient one and forms part of many belief systems, cultures and religions.

The practise of exorcisms began to decline in Western culture by the 18th century and was only rarely practiced until the latter half of the 20th century, at which time, due to media attention there was a 50% increase in the number of exorcisms being requested between the early 1960s and mid-1970s.

## THE CATHOLIC RITUAL OF EXORCISM

No one religion or lay would like to acknowledge the fact that Satan is alive and destroying souls in today's modern society. Many religions do not believe in possession and passionately discourage the belief that it may occur; throughout history , it seems that religions have had a deep-seated fear of Satan. However, it would appear from various form of literature, over many centuries would suggest that 'Fear' is Satan's greatest, and most powerful weapon. When someone fears Satan, and they believe he has more power over them than God, then he has power over them. Satan's biggest fear, is not exorcism, as is the popular belief, but confession. A priest who preaches and hears confessions in theory should be an ideal candidate to become an exorcist.

### The Procedure of Exorcism According to the Roman Ritual:

The Roman Ritual *'Rituale Romanum'* contains the longer rite of exorcism and states that the exorcist should, wear an alb and a purple stole, *'Superpelliceo et stola violacea undutus',* before the reciting the part of the prayer that begins *'Ecce crucem domine, fugite partes adversae'.* The priest is instructed to make the sign of the cross over the victim, and place the ends of the stole around the person's neck, *imponat extreman partesolae ejus'.*

It is acceptable for the priest to sew two normal sized stoles together to extend from his neck to the victims. This procedure can have an amazing effect of calming the victim in some cases, or inciting a violent reaction in others. It is believed that the stole not only symbolises, but demonstrates the power of the priesthood. Jesus is said to bind the evil spirits with the use of this sacramental.

The next part of the ritual instructs the priest to place his right hand on the head of the victim; this emulates Jesus laying hands on the sick to heal them. It has been documented that this process can have varying results, dependent on the priest and of course the victims. If an assistant priest is present at this ritual he too can place his hand on the victim's head at this point.

It is also stated that a Bible containing both the old and new testaments should be at hand when questioning and commanding the demons to respond.

The Rite of Exorcism uses the passages from John. 1:1-14; Mark 16:15-18; Luke 1:17-20; Luke 11:14-22 or whatever passage the Holy Spirit inspires. This can hasten along deliverance and yield many crucial answers towards the identity of the possessing demons. Many priests keep a collection of prayers on hand, the *'Raccolta'* is a popular example.

**John 1:1-17** In the beginning was the Word, and the Word was with God, and the Word was God.

**Mark 16:15-18** And He said to them, "Go into all the world and preach the gospel to every creature."

**Luke 17:1-20** Then said He unto the disciples, It is impossible but that offences will come: but woe unto him, through whom they come.

**Luke 11:14-22** Jesus was driving out a demon that was mute. When the demon left, the man who had been mute spoke, and the crowd was amazed.

The rules for exorcism state that the priest should have relics of the saints at hand. Not all relics are equal in worth. First class relics are to be preferred. The greater the sanctity of the saint the more powerful the cure.

**The St Benedict Medal** Can be pinned to the clothes of infants who are aggressive, pregnant women or anyone who feels they need protection from evil.

**The Rosary:** The use of the scapular of Our Lady of Mt Carmel and the Rosary are two sacramentals specifically mentioned in the Vatican ll document on the church *'Lumen Gentium'* The blessing of the rosary states, *Nos epireres de postate diaboli'* Our Lord Jesus Christ through his life, death and resurrection has 'snatched us from the power of the devil. Abundant graces are granted through proper recitation of the rosary. *'Ab omn hoste visbli et invisibilli et ubique in hoc saeculo liberetuir.'* (from every enemy both visible and invisible and everywhere in this lifetime be freed). St Dominic freed a heritic from 15,000 devils, when the man blasphemed the Blessed Mother and the Rosary. St Dominic preached on the fifteen mysteries of the rosary and asked the faithful to pray and meditate. For every mystery 1,000 demons left him in the form of burning coals until he was delivered. The Rosary is the chain that Our uses to bind Satan. It is often seen in a possessed person, that the demon is irritated and they complain that the rosary burns them and they often destroy the rosary.

**The Miraculous Medal** (Medal of the Immaculate Conception of Mary). While placing the medal around the neck, the priest prays, *'Ut piisima et imaculata caellorium Domini vos protegat atique defendat'* (Mat the Holy and Immaculate heavenly lady protect and defend you). Our Lady promises special graces to those who wear this medal around their neck. The same is true of the scapular, if worn with faith. 'They shall not suffer the eternal flames of Hell and shall be delivered from Purgatory on the Saturday after their death.

**The Crucifix** Should always be at hand. The victim will often stare at the cross and be forced to look away. The cross is symbolic of the defeat of Satan through the death of Christ. The prayer for Solemn Blessing of the Crucifix is then recited: *Ut quoties triumphum divinaw humnilitas, quae superbiam nostril hostris dejecit'* and (how often the divine humility has triumphed casting out the pride of our enemy). *Dignare respicere, bene +dicere et Sancti + fiacre hanc creatum incense, omnes languores, omnesque infirmitates, atque insidiar inimici, ororem ejus sentientes, effulgent, et separator a plasmate tuo; ut num quam laedatur amorsu antique serpentes'.* (Deign to care for bless and sanctity those being inflamed by passion and weakness, any sickness, deceits of the foe and suspicious felt by them. Be cast out and driven away from your creature)) and *'Numquain laedatur a morsu antique serpentis'* (Never to be hurt by the bite of the ancient serpent).

Below are selected paragraphs pertaining to the instruction of the Exorcist as shown in the Old Rite – Rules of the Roman Ritual of

Exorcism:

**Rule 1:** The priest who with the particular and explicit permission of his Bishop is about to exorcise those tormented by Evil Spirit, must have the necessary piety, prudence and personal integrity. He should perform this work heroic work humbly and courageously, not rely on his own strength, but on the power of God; and he must have no greed for material benefit, he should be of a mature age and be respected as a virtuous person.

**Rule 5:** Let the exorcist not for himself the tricks and deceits which evil spirits use in order to lead him astray. For they are accustomed to answering falsely. They manifest themselves only under pressure – in the hope that the exorcist will get tired and desist from pressuring them. Or they make it appear that the subject of the exorcism is not possessed at all.

**Rule 6:** Sometimes Evil Spirit betrays its presence, and then goes into hiding. It appears to have left the body of the possessed free from all molestation, so that the possessed thinks he is completely rid of it. But the exorcist should not, for all that desist until he sees the signs of liberation.

**Rule 10:** The exorcist must remember, therefore that Our Lord said there is a species of Evil Spirit which cannot be expelled except by prayer and fasting. Let him make sure that he and others follow the example of the Holy Father and make use of these two principle means of obtaining divine help and of repelling Evil Spirit.

**Rule 13:** He ought to have a crucifix at hand or somewhere in sight. If relics of the saints are available in a reverent way to the breast or the head of the person possessed (the relics must be properly and securely encased and covered). One will see to it that these sacred objects are not treated improperly or that no injury is done to them by the evil spirit. However, one should not hold the holy Eucharist over the head of the person or in any other way apply it to his body, owing to the danger of desecration.

**Rule 20:** During the exorcism the exorcist should use the words of the Bible rather than his own or somebody else's. Also, he should command Evil Spirit to state whether it is kept within the possessed because of some magical spell or sorcerer's symbol or some occult documents. For the exorcism to succeed the possessed must surrender them. If he has swallowed something like that, he will vomit it up. If it is outside his body in some place or other, Evil Spirit must tell the exorcist where it is. When the exorcist finds it he must burn it. In order for Satan to be driven out of the possessed, the exorcist must be humble. He must rely on God and only God for his answers and direction. Sometimes God forces the demon inside the possessed to reveal truths. However, the exorcist must be careful not to believe all that the demon possessing the victim might say. The demon will reveal exactly what the exorcist wants to hear though it is not the truth, in order to trick him. The exorcist out of his own curiosity, should not ask questions to the possessed regarding matters other than the exorcism at hand. Only through much prayer, fasting and humility of the exorcist along with the willingness of the victim, and of course the grace and Will of God, can one be freed of this affliction.

# The Amazing Saga of Florence Cook and Katie King

## Wayne Ridsdel

Florence Cook was born in the East End, in 1856, eight years after the Fox Sisters first introduced the world to the amazing world of Spiritualism. She was a normal child except for one account; she claimed that angels spoke to her. She led an otherwise unremarkable life until, aged 15, her parents held a séance with friends and family members. Here she was said to have become the focus of activity and to have obtained a table tilting at her first try. Of course many other séances followed and Florence became a medium to reckon with. Her specialty was creating 'spirit faces' while locked inside a homemade spirit cabinet (an invention of those famous mediums, the Davenport Brothers) and bound, hand, legs and neck, to a chair.

She soon gained a following; she was an attractive, well educated young woman with impeccable manners and, more importantly, she never charged anything for attending her séances, even refusing the gifts she was offered by her admirers. Of course the standard charge against mediums were brought up but did not harm her rise to stardom.

As her fame grew, so did her skills: she levitated, was tossed into the air by spirits and on one occasion an 'invisible force' tore off her dress. This contributed greatly to her popularity among Spiritualists and London thrill seekers.

At the time Florence was working as an assistant teacher in a girls school but her new found fame became a problem for the headmaster: parents started complaining that the girls had seen 'Strange things' happen around Florence and some even became worried that their children may somehow be affected by these unknown forces. The owner, a Mrs. Eliza Cliff, was forced to fire Florence to avoid damaging the reputation of the school though she obviously liked having the young woman around. In the end this is what probably allowed Florence's career to take off. Since she completely devoted herself to becoming a full-fledged medium.

## Katie King

During a séance held by Jonathon Koons at his Ohio, USA home in 1852 a mysterious spirit made his first appearance in the mortal world. He was once the dreaded privateer and sea captain Henry Owen Morgan who died in Jamaica in 1688 but, after reaching the afterlife, realized how wretched and horrible his existence had been and so he decided to atone for his sins by taking the new name John King and took unto himself the task of proving to humans the reality of the afterlife. John King went to become a great celebrity; he appeared in literally hundreds of séances and instructed the Davenport Brothers, those famous mediums, on how to build spirit cabinet. Jonathon Koons soon faded into nothingness (apparently he was caught cheating during a séance and this destroyed his already dubious reputation) but not before he introduced to the world a whole host of John King's relatives. The most famous was Annie Owen Morgan, the alleged daughter of the aforementioned privateer, who had now taken the identity of Katie. Like her father she wanted to atone for her sins (she claimed to have been an adulteress and a murderer) by proving to mortals the reality of the afterlife.

Katie King became every bit as famous as her father and her career lasted considerably longer, having appeared for the last time at a séance held in Rome in 1974 by the famous medium Fulvio Rendhell.

## Florrie Meets Katie

As Florence Cook's powers as a medium grew she became capable of producing more astounding and life-like pieces of materialization. In 1872 she produced a floating death-like pale face who claimed to be the famous Katie King. She had crossed the sands of time and the Atlantic Ocean to prove the reality of the afterlife in London to! It took Florence more than a year of strenuous efforts to produce a full body materialization of Katie. But in the meanwhile an accident threatened to cut Florence Cook's career as a medium short.

## Florence Cook and Katie King

On December 9, 1873 Florence was holding a séance for the Earl and Countess of Caithness and other selected guests. She produced a few full-body materializations before something highly unusual happened; An invited guest by the name of William Volkman jumped to his feet declaring Florence to be a fraud and he seized an 'apparition' by the wrist. Now, in the heyday of Spiritualism and mediumship it was considered highly inappropriate to touch an apparition, ectoplasm or a medium in a trance. According to popular lore this could cause the medium a serious trauma or even kill him/her.

Volkman tried to drag the apparition towards a source of light but the 'spirit' proved to be very corporeal and put up quite a fight, leaving Volkman with a bloody nose. The Earl of Caithness and other guests rushed to seize Volkman, allowing the spirit to make her escape. Volkman managed to free himself, rushed to the spirit cabinet and opened it, to reveal Florence still tied to the chair but with her clothing in disarray.

This could have proved disastrous to Florence Cook's career if not for one detail. Mr. Volkman was at the time engaged to Mrs. Samuel Guppy (the two married some months after this incident), a medium of wide renown who had developed a dislike for Florence. While skeptics had a field day, Florence was able to survive the ordeal without too much damage. But she knew very well that her reputation had to be spotless from then on.

Shortly after this incident Katie King began to appear fully materialized at Florence's séances. At the beginning she just nodded and smiled at those present but she quickly 'gained strength', walking among the sitters and offering them warm, very solid hands. It is at this point that her extraordinary resemblance with Florence Cook became apparent.

## Sir William Crookes: Physicist, Chemist and Spiritualist

At about this time Florence hears that the 'human wonder' Daniel Dunglas Home' was undergoing testing with a renowned London scientific researcher, William Crookes.

William Crookes, later Sir William Crookes, (1832-1919) is often remembered nowadays as the co-discoverer of the element thallium together with the Frenchman C.A. Lamy, but he was a very capable experimental physicist and chemist. His fame as a theorist never took up but he's still remembered to this day for the thoroughness and soundness of his experimental methods. He was on of the first researchers outside of Germany to embrace the new methods of spectography invented by Bunsen and Kirchoff and led the way in the rare earth studies. But he's also remembered for his involvement with 'supernatural' research. As said before he experimented with Daniel Dunglas Home shortly before this enigmatic man announced his retirement from the scenes.

### Sir William Crookes

Many scientists of renown, whose name are still held in the highest esteem nowadays investigated the reality of mediumship in the closing decade of the 19th century. Among the best remembered are Camille Flammarion, French astronomer, Alfred Russell Wallace, zoologist, botanist and father of zoogeography and William Fletcher, physicist and inventor.

Florence Cook had sent messages to William Crookes, asking him to be 'tested' using scientific methods. The great scientist answered enthusiastically and arranged for a séance to be held in his London home on the shortest possible term. During this séance Katie appeared, smiled at Crookes, took his hand and led him behind the curtain where Florence was laying motionless..

Crookes became sufficiently impressed to arrange for Florence Cook to come live in his house for an undetermined period of time to be 'studied' constantly. This period proved to be incredibly productive: Katie King agreed to appear in plain sight and Crookes took 44 photographs of her. All the originals were destroyed by Crookes' heirs shortly after his death and only a handful survive in copy form to this day. The most famous ones show Crookes standing arm in arm with Katie King, Katie appearing (though her face is conveniently obscured by an 'ectoplasmic shroud' next to an entranced Florence Cook and then the most famous and controversial of them all, the mirror sitter' photograph.

Crookes remained adamant that Florence Cook had passed every test to prove the reality of her powers and that he could vouch for her sincerity. But despite his stature as a researcher, he failed to convince the growing number of skeptics. The mirror sitter picture in particular has always been considered proof that something strange and not entirely clear was going on in the Crookes house.

Supporters of Crookes and Spiritualists instead were adamant about the reality of the phenomena, even going as far as claiming that Katie King appeared of her free will around the house outside of séances. This statement has never been substantiated by Sir William or Florence, so it should be taken with caution.

### Katie Must Go

In 1875 Katie King announced to an astonished audience that her time on Earth with Florence was coming to an end. The final goodbye was given at a private séance and Sir William affirmed that he witnessed Katie embracing Florence and bidding her goodbye for the last time. Immediately after Florence told Sir William that now there was no more need for her to stay: she married two months before and wanted to enjoy a little privacy away from the eyes of the public.

But the spirits were still calling her and in 1880 she came out of retirement with a new 'spirit guide', a ghost girl named Marie. Of course her supporters were delighted by her return but it was to be short-lived. In that same year, during a séance, Sir George Sitwell, a young and eccentric antiquarian and genealogist noticed corset stays under Marie's flowing white gown. He grabbed hold of her and ordered the lights to be lit. To the astonishment of everyone Florence Cook, the most revered medium of the time, had been caught cheating a séance.

This proved to be a scandal of enormous proportions and a serious blow to the credibility of spiritualism and mediums in general.

But again Florence's supporters again stood by her side, though in dwindling numbers. Yes she had been caught cheating but she did this only because her powers were disappearing and she didn't want to upset her supporters and lose her popularity. This was a standard defense and was used on a number of occasions, the most notable being the 'unmasking' of famous medium Eusapia Paladino (dubbed Madame Fakerino by the popular press) in 1909.

Florence's mainstream career was ruined but she continued to hold private séances for a few selected supporters and admirers until 1904, the year of her death.

Spiritualists claimed that she had produced again a number of genuine phenomena, witnessed by many reliable witnesses in full light, though the stature of these witnesses is not comparable to Sir Williams.

### The Aftermath

Sir William Crookes' academic career never suffered from his involvement with Florence Cook, but he was absolutely stunned by criticism from his colleagues. He was convinced of having followed the best procedures available and to have ruled out any possibility of fraud.

He remained a staunch supporter of Spiritualism and psychic research but ceased any active investigation. He was knighted in 1895 for his contributions to the advancement of physics and chemistry.

Katie King left Florence Cook but she didn't leave the mortal world; she appeared at a number of séances, the last one in 1974. If there ever was a spirit superstar, it was her. **So What Really Happened?** Like many other popular mediums before and after her, Florence Cook was elicited widely reactions. Supporters of Spiritualism have said that, yes she rigged a few séances but this was done not to upset her admirers at times when her powers were failing. Critics consider her an hoaxer, and a particularly good one; she was able to take in a famed and respected academic and to pass practically every test using her skills as an escape artist, and perhaps, with the help of an accomplice. But there may be more to it than that.

### Mirrir Sitter Photograph

One hypothesis says that Sir William Crookes and Florence Cook were lovers (though the former was married and the latter engaged at the time) and that this whole story was simply a rouse to cover their relationship, allowing the young woman to live with a married and respected member of society under the same roof.

Another, darker one, claim that Crookes may have been such an enthusiastic supporter of the Spiritualist cause that he willingly turned a blind eye on Florence or, much worse, that he became her accomplice. During Florence's stay, the Crookes hosted another, albeit much less popular, young medium in their mansion, named Mary Showers.

According to critics the two worked in tandem to perform their act: Florence donned a white flowing gown to become Katie King while Mary threw herself face down, or covered her face with a cloth or a fold of her dress to pretend to be entranced Florence, good manners dictating that a medium should never be touched while performing a materialization.

A very interesting detail is the resemblance between the medium and her 'spirit guide'. When comparing pictures of the two this is quite staggering, though both Crookes and other researchers pointed out a number of differences, like the hair colour (black for Florence and reddish for Katie), the ear lobes, (pierced for Florence not for Katie) and so on. Unluckily we are not able to make any of this out on the few pictures we have available and the two do look disturbingly similar.

Another argument against the reality of Florence Cook's powers is the set of photographs taken during Katie King's last appearance in 1974. While the medium (a middle-aged man at the time) cannot be accused of having donned a white gown and impersonated Katie King, one of the photographs clearly shows Katie holding hands with one of the sitters. Her face can be seen very clearly and she doesn't bear the slightest resemblance to the Katie King who used to appear at Crookes house.

# RIP

24$^{TH}$ February, 1860. This date is firmly etched in my memory. What I experienced that day has lived with me ever since. Not a day has passed where I haven't felt the confusion, fear and sheer desperation that descended on me on that fateful Thursday. For thirty years I have endured replays of torturous images when I least expect them. Tormenting cries echo round my head like the savage pangs of an eternal migraine, and all accompanied by the nauseating stench of what I can only call, rotting flesh and decay.

Come tomorrow, this has been my desolate and lonely existence for three terrible decades. I have long since rescinded all hope of escaping the merciless grip of whatever evil power has locked me forever in this ghastly prison. My last desperate hope is to reach out to the world from which I was plucked and pray for the knowledge that will exorcise these demons that have condemned and shackled me for so long without hope of reprieve.

My tale is harrowing, so I will be brief. I have no desire to inflict my unbearable misery on the unsuspecting soul who should bear witness to my dire plea for compassion and merciful salvation.

I sit here now, poised with pen in hand, eager to scribe, yet I am compelled to pause, for once again an impenetrable darkness is enveloping the room and a dozen voices surround me. Their inaudible chatter drones in my ears. A dozen voices speak all at once, yet not one can I single out to ease my frustration and hear what they say.

Prepare now, as I do, for my experience assures me that the images are about to manifest. The sickening smell of sulphur assaults my senses, and a bone-chilling coldness rises about my legs.

This terror is so familiar, it has attacked me with fearful regularity, yet still my being is rigid with panic. I beg for your company to offer me some comfort.

Its occurrence will be short, though I promise most sincerely; its haunting consequences will plague your sanity for years to come.

Like so many times before, I reach out my hand. My heart yearns for a supporting friend. Alas though, I am alone in this nightmare that has ensnared me.

But wait! What is this that manifests before me? It is not the fearsome demon that has appeared thus far.

What madness is this? Has my mind finally succumbed to the continual torment?

The image is formed ... and my father stands before me!

How can this be? My father died some fifteen years past.

Still he stands there, his hands out-stretched, beckoning me towards him. His face is shallow, translucent, as is common in ghosts.

The expression he wears causes me no fear. A smile lights his features, and fills my heart with childhood memories of the times I spent happily nestled in his lap, enjoying his fanciful stories and sharing his laughter.

The dozen voices have diminished. But one remains.

A woman's gentle words urge me to accept my dear father's beckoning.

"Take his hand," she calls. "Take his hand, he means you no harm. He has come to collect you and end your suffering."

Tempted as I am, my instincts scream out for me to resist.

Discarnate spirits are resourceful and cunning, they seek to trick gullible mortals into their world to feed and relish on their desirable earth-bound energy.

As I look at my father, his hand out-stretched and beckoning, I listen to the woman's compassionate narration. The realisation hits me; I hear no spirits, for the spirits are me.

The realm above me where my father resides and the realm below, where lives a gifted medium have combined to save me from my long-lived denial.

24th February, 1860 ... the day that I died.

Shed no tears for my poor lost soul, for now I have been redeemed and my wandering is ended.

Be of good cheer my friend, as I welcome my father's gesturing hand, and go to my rest, in peace and contentment, with my family and friends.

I bid you farewell and thank you for lending me a compassionate ear.

# Conducting an EVP session

EVP is one of the most used methods of investigation within the paranormal field.

EVP stands for Electronic voice phenomena, and this method involves using a sound recording device like a Dictaphone, doing a few voice recordings and listening back to see if any odd sounds are on the device while playing back, But how do you conduct this methods to the best ability?

First keep in mind, the Older and cheaper the Voice recorder the more likely you will capture odd sounds,this may be due to the quality and the way it's built.

The more expensive the recorder the less chance you will have capturing sounds "studio quality"

<u>Here are lee steers notes on conducing EVPS</u>

$\frac{35}{17}$ If you don't want false EVPS then I would recommend the "brand" Zoom for voice recorders, which are studio quality.

$\frac{35}{17}$ Test your microphone before the investigation / evp session, and set the desired volume and recording level "higher record volume will = more evps"

$\frac{35}{17}$ Get a pen and paper, and take note of your surroundings and possible interactions "We are in an old wood cabin, late at night, Next to a road, there's Birds in the trees," This is so if you have any evps upon review you have notes on what was around that area, You may hear a sound like a growl, You check your notes and see it says "Car Passing 0:22"

30

$\frac{35}{17}$ Designate someone to be an **Interaction Caller**, While in evp mode this person would shout out any interactions they hear, it is very important to TAG, all sounds heard with your own ears, which aren't paranormal, as on review you may think its paranormal.

$\frac{35}{17}$ Start the EVP Session, by Saying date, time, location and get everyone to say their names who's present, Try to take it in turns of asking questions, allowing 10 – 20 seconds gap per question for an answer.

$\frac{35}{17}$ End the evp Session, buy saying end of evp session

$\frac{35}{17}$ Use headphones to review on site if you wish or on laptop when home, I recommend reviewing on site with good headphones.

$\frac{35}{17}$ If any evps are caught revert back to your notes to see if any interactions could have caused it.

$\frac{35}{17}$ Remember the human hearing hertz is 20+ voice recorders will be slightly lower.

$\frac{35}{17}$ Share your evp with the paranormal magazine.

# Ghost Hunters 10th season premiere featured
## Gettysburg, Pa. Locations

### By Jeffrey B. Roth

GETTYSBURG, Pa. – The SyFy network paranormal team, Ghost Hunters, spent several days investigating Gettysburg locations – the Jennie Wade House, the Farnsworth House, a portion of the battlefield and the Haunted Orphanage, (Homestead Orphanage), in late last September.

1990 view of the Georgia McClellan residence. The fatal bullet pierced the door visible in the left side wall. The likeness of Jennie is from an old photograph.

The premiere episode of the 10th season of Ghost Hunters, featured investigations and from all four locations. Dwayne Pope, a tour guide, with Ghostly Images, who worked with the television production team. Ghostly Images, of Gettysburg Ghost Tours, owns both the Jennie Wade and Homestead Orphanage locations.

"They've never been here before," Pope said. "The production crew were there for about a week. Jason Hawes, Steve Gonsalves and Dave Tango were there for two days. They investigated the Cashtown Inn a couple of years ago."

Gettysburg, Pope said, is considered to be one of the most haunted towns in the U.S. About two years ago, Haunted History, a production of the History 2 network, (H2), investigated both locations. That episode aired last season.

Gettysburg paranormal expert and author, Mark Nesbitt, was contacted by Ghost Hunters alerting him that they intended to do investigations in town. Nesbitt met the Ghost Hunter team about 6 years ago in a conference held in Richmond, Va.

"Are there any child spirits remaining in Gettysburg and why?" Nesbitt said, explaining that was the focus they intended for the episode. "I had done an investigation of the Jennie Wade House and Farnsworth House in 1991 with Karyol Kirkpatrick, (psychic who had been on Maury Povich), and DJs Cooke and Crockett for a Halloween Special. Evidence from the Wade House was that there was an 'unfinished mourning' going on, (Kirkpatrick's very first impression). We went through the house and as we were leaving the basement the chain between the visitor's area and the body on the table began to swing when no one was near it. Karyol said, 'Oh, that's Jennie's father.' It suddenly dawned on me that he had been incarcerated when she was killed and indeed could not properly mourn."

The Jennie Wade House, named after the only civilian to die during the Battle of Gettysburg, was named by the Travel Channel as the sixth most haunted house in America and the most haunted building in Gettysburg," Pope said. "The Jennie Wade House has been featured on Ghost Adventures, Ghost Lab, Ghost Finders, Most Haunted Live, Haunted History on the History 2 Network, CBS Radio and a local television station, WPMT Fox 43. Visitors to the Jennie Wade House have experienced items in the home moving inexplicably, noises, footsteps, orbs, voices, the scent of bread baking in the kitchen and full body apparitions. Reports of unexplained activity are shared on a nearly daily basis."

The orphanage was named in an article featured in the USA Today, as one of the top ten creepiest places in the United States to visit, Pope said. The orphanage has also played host to Ghost Adventures, Ghost Lab, Ghost Finders, Haunted History on the History 2 Network, CBS Radio and local television station WPMT Fox 43.

"I investigated the Homestead Orphanage, (Soldiers' National Museum),with a Canadian film crew several years back, before it was 'haunted,'" Nesbitt said. "I read off the names of some of the orphans and got some answers via electronic voice phenomena (EVP). Jason and Steve brought some pretty good evidence to me. The figure they caught on the FLIR camera was impressive. You couldn't see it very well on TV but it seemed to partially float, (no obvious leg movement), at first. They tried to debunk it, (good technique), with a living person and the results were obviously different. The other visual evidence was a shadow that appeared that looked immediately to me like a hoop skirt, (though, once again, I couldn't see it on TV). There were a couple of noises that did sound like voices, (not EVP because they heard them live), and I heard them too. But there were a couple they had recorded, but I heard nothing and so they were left out of the show. All in all I was impressed with most of what they got, the EVP and video more that actual sounds that they heard and recorded because, as you know, on Baltimore Street it can get pretty noisy outside--people going by, trucks, etc."

"Visitors to the orphanage also share their experiences, including but not limited to items moving, noises, voices of children, toys in the cellar being moved around, orbs, foul odors and full body apparitions of children," Pope said. "These unexplained phenomena are also reported on a nearly daily basis."

Last year Nesbitt published Civil War Ghost Trails, (Stackpole Publishers), about all the major battlefields and he's working with Katherine Ramsland, expert on forensics, former consultant on "CSI" and "Bones" doing the second in the series called "Haunted Crime Scenes."

"We started our own 'Second Chance Publications' and are publishing my own stuff," Nesbitt said. "I'm also doing paranormal investigation weekends with the Cashtown Inn and James Gettys Hotel."

In 1866, the National Homestead at Gettysburg, was opened as an orphanage and a home for widows. Located on Baltimore Street, adjacent to Cemetery Hill. It was founded to honor Amos Humiston, a Union sergeant with New York 154th Regiment, known as the "Hardtack" regiment, who was killed on the first day of the battle, July 1, 1863. About a week later, near York and Stratton streets, Humiston's body was discovered. Grasped in his hand was an ambrotype, an early type of photograph, depicting his three children – Frank, 8; Alice, 6; and Freddie, 4.

A Philadelphia physician, Dr. John Francis Bourns, tried to identify Humiston's body. During the Civil War, soldiers were not issued dog tags as they are today. As a result of the publicity, some time in mid-November, Hunston was identified. As a result of the publicity, Bourns was able to raise money to found the orphanage for the children of Union soldiers, killed during the war.

Within 12 years of its opening, the orphanage closed as a result of a scandal involving allegations that the orphanage matron, Rosa Carmichael, allegedly abused children. According to news coverage of the day, Carmichael had created a dungeon in the basement, where she shackled some children. Bourns, who was responsible for founding the orphanage, was also accused of embezzling a large amount of funds from the Homestead, according to historical records.

In connection with the Ghost Hunters investigation, operators of both buildings are offering combination tours. The tours will be available, on Saturdays, beginning January 25 and running through March 1. The price is $13 per person.

For more information, visit **https://www.facebook.com/GhostlyImagesofGettysburg**.

**Ghosts of Gettysburg** website.

**Jeff**

# Drakelow Tunnels
# Shadow Factory

The Drakelow Tunnels are a former underground military complex beneath the Kingsford Country Park north of Kidderminster, Worcestershire, covering 250,000 sq ft. The tunnels, which have a total length of 3.5 miles, have a very interesting past and are a historical monument to the military history of the United Kingdom.

Designed by Sir Alexander Gibb & Partners, the Drakelow Tunnel Complex (originally called "Drakelow Underground Dispersal Factory") was excavated during World War II in sandstone hills near the village of Kinver and the town of Kidderminster. It was originally constructed as a shadow factory for the Rover car company who were at the time manufacturing engines for the Bristol Aeroplane Company. It was also intended to supply components to Rover's main shadow factories at Acocks Green and Solihull, to supply spare parts, and to act as a backup facility if either of the main shadow factories was damaged by enemy action. The tunnels contained dormitories, storage areas, workshops, electrical equipment, toilets, offices, a BBC studio, a GPO Telephones communications facility and other facilities.

During the 1950's and the growing Cold War, the site was initially used by the Ministry of Supply for storage. Then around 1958 part of the site was developed by the Home Office as a Regional Seat of Government (RSG9). It was publicly exposed in a demonstration held there by the West Midlands Committee of 100 in the summer of 1963. Under later Home Defense schemes the bunker was designated a Sub-Regional Control (SRC), Sub-Regional Headquarters (SRHQ) and finally Regional Government Headquarters (RGHQ). The site was greatly modernized in the early 1980's, only a small portion of the site was designated for use. New blast doors were fitted in place of the previous wooden factory doors and the interior of the site was refurbished in the areas forward of tunnel 4.

It is claimed that during construction workers were crushed to death by collapsing tunnels and accidents with dumper trucks. Reports of experiments gone wrong, and people stationed there taking their own lives. Many mediums have picked up on a deadly demon's presence down by the old theatre.

# My home, The Cage St Osyth

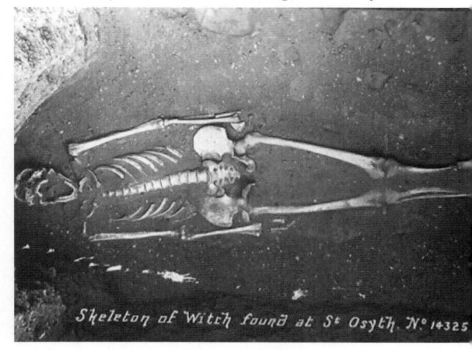

Skeleton of Witch found at St Osyth. Nº 14325

### Moving In Day

The day went relatively smoothly and by dark we had got most of our belongings in the house , minus sofas and beds but we did have a mattress to put on the floor for sleeping that night and we could sit on boxes for the evening.

That first evening I was in the kitchen looking out of the window on to the alley at the back of the cage,  it's called Coffin alley as it was used to bring the dead from the church at one side of the village to the cemetery where they would be laid to rest on the other side of the village via coffin alley and past The cage, I was all of a sudden acutely aware of someone behind me, I turned around and there a saw a tall dark male  figure walking through the Cage room into the front room..it was the first time of many I would see that male figure along with others..women and children in my stay of 3 years in The Cage.

I realised very soon on that the house I had bought, the house I was supposed to start my new happy life in came with some very serious activity of a paranormal nature the which of like I didn't ever realise or understand could happen. As I recall it pretty much started straight away, with little things at first like taps always running, doors slamming or opening with no wind to push or pull them, footsteps upstairs and women talking or whispering but you could never quite make out what they were saying. The house was alive when it shouldn't have been, when we were in bed upstairs late at night, downstairs you could hear the house live on, in its very strange disturbing way.

The daylight hours in The cage were no less active than the night hours…ornaments would fly of the mantel piece, the old chain from the original prison building would swing back and forward as if to remind me of the horrific history of my home and the hall stairs door would crash open in a forceful almost violent way, blood splatters appeared in the hall in broad daylight in front of witnesses apart from myself. The TV sound would go up and down with no one near the controls to adjust them and you would hear someone pacing back and forth in the upstairs hall …it didn't stop it was all the time and there was nothing I could do.

One day in the afternoon to my utter amazement a ghost lady walked from the prison room into my front room where I was sitting on the floor …she came over and was carrying some kind of oval wooden bowl, she took something out of the bowl that looked like herbs or leaves and sprinkled them over my head in silence…I was totally transfixed and stunned and I dare not breath but she didn't terrify me..she felt kind and good.  I just sat in shock at what was happening, I knew it was real and that I wasn't dreaming or seeing things,  she was there in a see through kind of colour , she didn't say who she was but I felt she was one of those poor women incarcerated in my house for witch craft before her execution many years before

I feel the spirits that are still existing in The Cage  or at least some of them became more comfortable with us being there as they became more bold if you like about what they did and the activity in the house, for example  one hot sunny summer day I was sitting in the front room with the back door open which incidentally  was directly opposite me when I saw a handsome young man with jet black long  hair and wild rugged looks floating in the hall staring at me intently through the wooden beams, I saw the lines on his face and thought his skin looked older than he was.  He was there for a good 30 seconds plus, and he was moving very slowly but he saw me and I saw him and we both knew it.

As the months rolled on my flatmate Nicole left to move in with her boyfriend  and sadly I was left to face the house alone in the day and the night. One morning I was brushing my teeth getting ready for work when I got hit so hard on my bum as I was bending over the sink, it hurt so much and  was such a shock I screamed chucking the toothbrush in the air with toothpaste flying everywhere…I was totally stunned I lived alone no one was there.  On another occasion I was pushed when I was standing in the top hall way, other times I would be sitting there and witness objects whizz across the room.   Over time i learnt how to live with this Haunting  the best possible way I knew how, I couldn't leave the house as I was in dept with the mortgage and had to work very long and hard to make the monthly payments because at that time the interest rates had pretty much doubled, so had my mortgage which put me in a position where I was completely trapped by the house and financially.

I would lie in bed at night hearing them come up the stairs and watching in abject fear as my bedroom door latch rattled as if someone was trying to open the door to come in, but didn't...the door didn't open but he/they was there alright, the other side of the door making the latch rattle scaring me half to death.

As the time rolled on I met a man and became pregnant with my son Jesse, Jesses dad stayed with me in The Cage for a time but the relationship was no good so he didn't stay long so I found myself left in the house once again with a baby alone, now it was even harder to escape. One day I was ironing downstairs this, was rare for me to be downstairs at this point because for many months I had lived in my bedroom upstairs, I would get in from work with jess, walk in the door then straight up the stairs to my bedroom which looked over to the pub next door, I liked it because I could see and hear normal life outside and it game me comfort knowing the other side of the window things were ok. I would stay in that room all night, In essence I was too scared to sit downstairs or have any contact with the house itself if you know what I mean, I was hiding from what the house was and who was in it with me. Anyway I was ironing when I saw Jesses little toys start moving across the floor and playing their music by themselves as If a little child was playing with them, and I just knew what was happening so I panicked turned off the iron and ran to get upstairs quick. I opened the stairs door and went to take the first step up when saw a man standing at the top of the landing with modern day cloths on...he wasn't a burglar he was a ghost of a man and standing very near my sons cot......i knew then that no matter what or how hard it was I had to escape from that house for me and my baby son.

The day I left I felt like the house had won, I looked around one last time standing by the door, just about to step out and leave and I heard the growl I had heard many times before, a dark hostile noise that didn't like me and that wanted me gone. The house had won but I didn't care I just needed to feel safe again in a home, somewhere I can relax watching TV or not to be too scared to go to the loo in the middle of the night, just those little things people take for granted.

That is the very short version of a few of my experiences of my 3 years living in The Cage and the subsequent following 6 years of owning it and unrevealing the History and secrets of The Cage, where some of my questions have been answered., I can assure you it is a compelling and horrifying story at the same time. I am currently writing a book of my experiences living with this horrific modern day haunting and the historical facts behind the Haunting called THE CAGE A Modern Day Haunting BY VANESSA MITCHELL so if you are curious to know the whole story you soon can.....if you're brave enough........

# wiccan foods

I wrote this article because I found this topic interesting i compiled a few products that I've read upon .
These are staple and ordinary foods that you probably already have in your pantry or refrigerator, but maybe you never realized that they contained magical properties before. This information can be different to other people, but that's because eventually you will find your own magical path.

I will start with an **Apple**. known as the a Wiccan food that's a sacred fruit to the Goddess. And also The sacred fruit to the Isle of Avalon. Avalon is the place where King Arthur was taken after fighting Mordred at the Battle of Camlann to recover from his wounds.
If you cut an apple horizontally through it's centre, you will see the 5 pointed star formed by its seeds. It's a wiccan food that is used in love, healing, garden magic, and immortality.

This one i found interesting **Bacon**. It's a meat that's ruled by Adonis. Adonis is a god of beauty and desire, and is a central figure in various mystery religions. Bacon when used as a Wiccan food can be eaten to increase earnings. Can be smeared on the body to remove marital tension and to aid in the forgiveness of adulterous affairs.
Basil is another popular food for Wicca in the kitchen. A very useful and fragrant herb that can be used fresh or dried in cooking. This herb is a lust herb and the aroma calls forth sexual energy. When i started to read upon basil and its magical properties i found that Basil was used in English folk magic, like so many other things, to ward off harmful spells as well as to keep away pests.

Also, several sources say that if a gift of basil is given to a member of the opposite sex, he or she will fall deeply in love with the giver and be forever faithful. In Romania, this act is representative of an official engagement.
by Philip Williams
**Redridge**

# Vernal Equinox, 20<sup>th</sup> March 2014

The coming equinox is one of two and it is the result of the the Earth's equator being in line with the centre of the Sun. At this point the earth is not tilting away or towards the Sun. Because of this occurrence night and day at the equator are around equal length and this is probably the reason why they call it an Equinox as the word derives from Latin meaning Equal Night.

The approaching equinox also takes the name of Spring Equinox and so indicates the first day of Spring. After this day the North pole begins to lean towards the Sun giving us a period of longer daylight.

Many ancient cultures around the world have celebrated this day in many different ways. For example the Mayans in Mexico built a huge stone pyramid in such a way that twice a year at the equinoxes of spring and winter the setting sun makes a light display that resembles a snake moving slowly down the pyramid. You can observe many countries across the world and witness old traditions fading into new trends but nearly all countries had their own way of celebrating the coming of a new year. In Germany you will see the Easter bunnies and the chocolate eggs but you will also find people letting in the spring with a bonfire and taking part in family reunions and other activities with long standing tradition.

At this time of year the ancients would have held these festivals also for their gods and goddesses for instance in Egypt it would be Hathor, Cyprus Aphrodite and Ostara of Scandinavia. With the Celtic people some would worship the Green Man and Mother Earth both of which would explain some of the traditions they took part in. To honor the Green Man the leader of the hunt we may still take part in an Easter egg hunt, to symbolise and honour the feminine energy of mother earth fertility rites would take place and rituals to symbolise new beginnings and fresh starts.

Today many of us may take part in practices that date back to some of the earliest times of man's understanding without realising it. We have the sharing of Easter eggs, eggs the symbol of new life in spring. You have spring cleaning to symbolise fresh new starts. The sharing of Easter cards can even be found in old Italian traditions where people would write their names on pieces of paper then pick them from a bowl and would partner up with each other for the year.

This Easter no matter what you do we hope you enjoy this time of year, you may even start your own practices to pass on to the next generation.

# Interview

## Alexandra Holzer
### The Daughter Of Paranormal
### Investigating, Hans Holzer

### By Pamela Wellington

I have been fascinated with mediums for a long time, and believe
that there are true mediums out there. Mediums have an ancient history, and
there are many sources to learn about the history of mediums, so I will not be
writing about it's history. Rather, I will deal with it's nature, its sources,
it's kinds and its various manifestations in the 21st century.

I am very happy to include an interview which I conducted in January of 2014,
via email, with Alexandra Holzer, the daughter of the father of paranormal
investigating, Hans Holzer. I think that readers will find her comments very
enlightening and intellectually challenging.

Medium-ship is the practice of intervening, moderating, arbitrating,
interceding the communication between spirits of the dead and human beings.
Attempts to contact the dead date back to early human history, with medium-ship
gaining in popularity during the 19th century. The practice still continues to
this day.

In recent years, scientific research has been undertaken to ascertain the
validity of claims of medium-ship. Experiments which have seemingly found
evidence of paranormal activity have been criticized by scientists for not
establishing thorough test conditions. This is the basic, on-going problem with
trying to prove the paranormal. The tests themselves are usually called into
question for faulty scientific method or other and various problems with
procedure. Believers don't require proof. Skeptics will not be swayed by proof.
That leaves those of us in the middle; what I call the seekers of truth. We
neither believe nor dis-believe. We seek, experiment, investigate, research, and
formulate hypothesis.

There are several different variants of medium-ship; the best known forms are
where a spirit takes control of a medium's voice and uses it to relay a message,
or where the medium simply 'hears' the message and passes it on. Other forms
involve manifestations of the spirit, such as apparitions or the presence of a
voice, and telekinetic activity.

Some mediums claim that they can listen to and relay messages from spirits, or that they can allow a spirit to control their body and speak through them directly or by using automatic writing or drawing. Medium-ship is often classified into two main categories: "mental" and "physical":

Mental mediums tune in to the spirit world by listening, sensing, or seeing spirits or symbols.
Physical mediums are believed to produce materialization of spirits, objects, and other effects such as knocking, rapping, bell-ringing, etc.

During seances, mediums are said to go into trances, varying from light to deep, that permit spirits to control their minds. Medium-ship also forms part of the belief-system of some New Age groups. In this context, and under the name "channelling", it refers to a medium who receives messages from a "teaching-spirit".

Attempts to communicate with the dead have been documented back to early human history. The story of the Witch of Endor tells of one who raised the spirit of the deceased prophet Samuel to allow the Hebrew king Saul to question his former mentor about an upcoming battle, as related in the First Book of Samuel in the Old Testament Bible.

"Mental mediumship" is communication of spirits with a medium by telepathy. The medium mentally "hears" (clairaudience), "sees" (clairvoyance), and/or feels (clairsentience) messages from spirits. Directly or with the help of a spirit guide, the medium passes the information on to the message's recipient. When a medium is doing a reading for a particular person, that person is known as the "sitter."

Trance medium-ship

Trance medium-ship is often seen as a form of mental medium-ship.

Most trance mediums remain conscious during a communication period, wherein a spirit uses the medium's mind to communicate. The medium allows their ego to step aside for the message to be delivered. At the same time, one has awareness of the thoughts coming through.

In a typical deep trance, the medium may not have clear recall of all the messages conveyed while in an altered state; such people generally work with an assistant. That person writes down or otherwise records the medium's words.

Physical medium-ship

Physical medium-ship is defined as manipulation of energies and energy systems by spirits. This type of medium-ship is claimed to involve things that an ordinary person can perceive, such as loud raps and noises, voices, materialized objects, materialized spirit bodies, or body parts such as hands, legs and feet. The medium is used as a source of power for such spirit manifestations.

## Direct voice

Direct voice communication is the claim that spirits speak independently of the medium, who facilitates the phenomenon rather than produces it. The role of the medium is to make the connection between the physical and spirit worlds. This form of medium-ship also permits the medium to participate in the discourse during seances, since the medium's voice is not required by the spirit to communicate.

## Channeling

In the later half of the 20th century, Western medium-ship developed in two different ways. One type involves psychics or sensitives who speak to spirits and then relay what they hear to their clients.The other incarnation of non-physical medium-ship is a form of channeling in which the channeler goes into a trance, or leaves their body. He or she allows the spirit-person to borrow his/her body, who then talks through them. In the trance, the medium enters a cataleptic state marked by extreme rigidity. As the control spirit takes over, the medium's voice may change completely. The spirit answers the questions of those in its presence.

## Psychic senses

Psychic senses used by mental mediums are sometimes defined differently than in other paranormal fields. A medium is said to have psychic abilities but not all psychics function as mediums. The term clairvoyance, for instance, may be used to include seeing spirits and visions instilled by spirits. The Parapsychological Association defines clairvoyance as information derived directly from an external physical source.

Clairvoyance or "clear seeing", is the ability to see anything that is not physically present.
Clairaudience or "clear hearing", is defined as the ability to hear the voices or thoughts of spirits.
Clairsentience or "clear sensing", is the ability to have an impression of what a spirit wants to communicate, or to feel sensations instilled by a spirit.
Clairsentenence or "clear feeling" is a condition in which the medium takes on the ailments of a spirit, feeling the same physical problem which the spirit person had before death.
Clairalience or "clear smelling" is the ability to smell a spirit.
Clairgustance or "clear tasting" is the ability to receive taste impressions from a spirit.
Claircognizanse or "clear knowing", is the ability to know something without

receiving it through normal or psychic senses. It is a feeling of "just knowing

## Scientific skepticism

Many skeptics believe that medium-ship can be explained by the power of suggestion and telepathy and that there is no clear evidence for spirit communication. Scientists who study anomalistic psychology (the study of human behavior and experience connected with the paranormal, without the assumption that there is anything paranormal involved.) consider medium-ship to be the result of fraud or psychological factors. Research from psychology for over a hundred years has revealed that where there is not fraud, medium-ship can be explained by hypnotism, magical thinking or suggestion. Trance medium-ship, which is claimed to be caused by spirits speaking through the medium have been proven in cases to be alternate personalities from the medium's subconscious. This theory, however, must be disregarded, since, in this decade, the psychiatric community has debunked most multiple personality disorder diagnoses as false or faked. The medium may also obtain information about their sitters by a technique called cold reading and obtain information from the sitter's behavior, clothing and body language.

Let me say here that, like all paranormal phenomena, it can and does get faked. Fraud exists in the paranormal community. I think we can, unfortunately, all agree to that. However, unlike the so-called scientists, who tend to discount all paranormal phenomena as a product of crazy minds, magical thinking or fraud, we all know that there are real psychics, real paranormal phenomena, real mystery in this world that defies logic and reason, and also defies, so far, any attempt to nail it down and prove it, yet. I say yet because I am on a quest to document the reality of spiritual phenomena, someday. So, even though I include the doubters and skeptics' theories in this article, I am not a skeptic. I am neither a believer. I am in the middle: I am a seeker of truth.

For wisdom on the subject, here is an email interview with Alexandra Holzer, daughter of Hans Holzer.

Here are Alexandra's unedited comments on the subject of mediums:

Question: What is medium-ship, in your opinion?

Alexandra: In my opinion, Mediumship is the ability to foresee tapping into various high-levels of happenings for many individual lives and natural environments. For instance, a good medium can know personal information about a stranger or who is around them without ever knowing them. They can help solve crimes with police departments. They can read people and environments to create a visual map so-to-speak, to help whomever is in need. It takes up a lot of time and energy to cultivate this ability, to deliver as much accuracy and helpful information for the seeker. There are many titles and meanings in the ability to utilize what we all have from birth, our sixth sense, to go beyond the veil and realms into the deep layers of the spiritual world. We're so attached to the idea of the 'physical,' that there is a science to this in which we know that how the universe is constructed with the laws, forces, and constants of the universe. It always ends up to showcase life, implying intelligence existed prior to matter. With that in mind, how can one dismiss one's claim to this extraordinary perception that goes beyond some individuals abilities? Not all of us are open enough or even gifted enough to hone in on this natural tool if you will, to enhance our experience here while on earth. According to Dr. Robert Lanza, he says, "If the body generates consciousness, then consciousness dies when the body dies. But if the body receives consciousness in the same way that a cable box receives satellite signals, then of course consciousness does not end at the death of the physical vehicle. In fact, consciousness exists outside of constraints of time and space. It is able to be anywhere: in the human body and outside of it. In other words, it is non-local in the same sense that quantum objects are non-local."

Lanza also believes that multiple universes can exist simultaneously. In one universe, the body can be dead. And in another it continues to exist, absorbing consciousness which migrated into this universe. This means that a dead person while traveling through the same tunnel ends up not in hell or in heaven, but in a similar world he or she once inhabited, but this time alive. And so on, infinitely. It's almost like a cosmic Russian doll afterlife effect." He has stirred up this long-time controversy as my father (Dr. Hans Holzer) has researched then written about that very theory that life does exist after-life and indeed holds scientific merit. The notion that life does not end when the body dies, and that it can last forever is what we have always looked at in the scientific community but in the Metaphysical community, we have always believed without the hard based facts as a spiritualist would feel. Feeling is also part of the life and death scenario and cannot be dismissed nor can one seeing and hearing the dead as the living. Dr. Robert Lanza was voted the 3rd most important scientist alive by the NY Times, and has no doubts that this is possible.

Question: What kind of medium are you?

Alexandra: I'm an Intuitive Empath and so I feel deeply for others such as human, animal and for our environment. I wear my heart on my sleeve and can use my intuitive meters to figure out people and places without knowing too much data.

Question: How did your father test mediums?

Alexandra: My father believed and wrote that it was a 50/50 accuracy when testing mediums or psychics in his lair at his Manhattan office. Today, I may disagree with that number but I do believe that there is arise if one of such abilities claims they are all knowing and can never be wrong in their foretelling. That's just plain hogwash and I won't stand for it. When he tested the mediums, he would ask questions, write on cards and then perform tests to see how accurate they were and gave them a score. Over all he was impressed by many and this helped him in his research to further use in his studies how mediums and psychic function brain wise and emotion wise. He knew there was something greater then us all at work with those individuals that could come up with such information, back before the internet may I remind your readers, where no-one could do a google search and within one minute have personal information! Such mediums like Sybil Leek, Manhattan's Eileen Garret and Yoloana Bard who helped Actor Kelsey Grammar plus my old time family friend Marissa Anderson, still at it who helped the Mercando Family. This was a case in Brooklyn, New York, a long time ago with my father. They were the duo that went to that haunted home to get answers and answers they got! SyFy aired the reenactment of this case but cut out both my father and Marissa's role on it who were the ones who worked on that case! So I am setting that record straight if I may.

Question: What is your opinion of the field of paranormal investigating today? If you have read any of the articles in my blog, you know that I am disturbed by many trends in the field which abandon standards, integrity, and any sort of scientific method, as well as any spirituality that insists upon goodness, honesty and a caring spirit. So, I tend to go after what I see to be wrong with things going on. What are your feelings about today's 21st century practice of medium-ship, psychics and the field of paranormal investigating?

Alexandra: I've answered these types of questions before and I've come to the conclusion to just say this: It's quite obvious what the trends are for and who they attract. Anyone who has a shred of dignity, an ounce of self-respect or ability as a researcher will not associate themselves with that garbage. It has it's place, yes, as with anything else in life. But, just because it has found a place, doesn't mean I want to frequent it!

Question: Is there a substantive difference between female and male mediums?

Alexandra: No. Gender doesn't play a role in whether or not one has the ability to be a medium or psychic. There is the assumption that men are generally less emotional towards situations then woman, and there may be some merit there as the two sexes are very different. However, what sex they are should have no bearing on how they perform to help those in need with the other side.

Question: In your experience and opinion, what percentage of mediums are fakes or frauds and how many are the real deal?

Alexandra: I don't have a number percentage wise but I feel that it would be equal to both as there are good ones, there are bad ones. For instance let's talk about the labeling used more so today then back in the day. Some try to call themselves this or that to separate themselves out from their peers but overall, you just need to know what your own ability is and run with that. If you can't hear the dead but see them, then that's your ability while another person may be able to hear them just not see them when describing details. I am sure I am missing some but there is Psychic-Medium, Channeler, Intuitive, Clairaudient, Clairvoyant, Clairsentient or just plain Psychic, all for being 'all-knowing.'

Question: Anything else you would like to add?

Alexandra: As far as medium-ship goes, it's an individual experience and no-one can take that away from you, not the skeptic or the negative nelly. You need to be an independent when it comes to this field and work with many to fully comprehend what exactly is it...that we are seeking? Knowledge is truly the power and we are given such little time here, why not make the best with it and be helpful not hurtful. Let's grow up please and stop the name calling shall we? Kindergarten is over, adults need to behave as such and the behavior especially being recorded on-line, has no place in a field in which I personally grew up in and have the merit to say as such.

Me: Thank you so much for your help.

Alexandra: My pleasure. :)

... We have a comic book novel series coming out by March I believe, will have to confirm and I've just completed my second children's book and working on a film by my father's from the 90s. Dan Aykroyd came out with another great telling of how my father was the best and I will leave that quote and link here...

LINK: http://www.childmind.org/en/press/brainstorm/dan-aykroyd-credits-autism-helping-him-make-ghostb

"One of my symptoms included my obsession with ghosts and law enforcement—I carry around a police badge with me, for example. I became obsessed by Hans Holzer, the greatest ghost hunter ever. That's when the idea of my film Ghostbusters was born."

Dan Aykroyd.

All my best,

-Alexandra

**My blog, titled: What The Phenomena:**
http://pjwellingtonwtph.blogspot.com/

## Ghost Gallery

The following photographs are from my own gallery and I wanted to share them to those who have an interest in the paranormal, all photographs were taken by myself and have not been tampered with, as an avid fan of all things spooky I was impressed with these and thought id share them to like minded fans. I hope you get some insights into the other world through these photos and to make up your own mind about them. Enjoy..

**Helen Cherry**

## Lifting Spirits

Throughout the years,(30)to be exact I have encountered many encounters, in which society calls paranormal. I feel these started to occur after facing a near death experience at the age of 10 and increased at the age

of 21,once again facing a near death experience. Since the age of 10,I started to realize that the individuals that I was seeing , were not of the living.

I also started to hear and feel the presence of those who had already passed. Every residence I resided in there were many encounters that I faced with friends,family and my children witnessing as well.

I felt this was normal ,that everyone went through this on a daily basis until it started to affect everyone that would visit my homes,and this lead to not many wanting to visit.

I decided to become a paranormal investigator and take groups on guided paranormal investigations,to teach them how to use the equipment and to help prove that the spiritual world does exist. During these investigations, people would notice the increased paranormal activity that would occur when I was present. I still just thought this was normal, Nothing out of the ordinary.

Until people began to show me photographs ,for me to review and look for paranormal activity within. I then noticed I was receiving more information from these photographs that I would have ever known.I spoke to the local church and was told that I am a medium.

My husband and I are Lifting Spirits Paranormal Society and our goal is to help prove the spiritual world does exist

**"Paranormal magazine contacted Lifting spirits back asking if they would like para mag to show any photos they have caught"**

Hello, this is Carla's husband Daniel. Thank you so much for this opportunity! Carla told me that you would like to feature some of our pictures in the write up as well, and that's great.

The first one that I will send, was featured on coast to coast am! It is what we believe to be the spirit of Jennie Wade! Because of her gifts, Carla captured this amazing photograph within 5 minutes of being on the Jennie wade house tour in Gettysburg, Pa.! She was being told to take the picture's in the mirror.

The Above picture is of an angel looking in through the bridge. She is watching, and protecting us. You can even see what resembles a crown on her head!

Now, I chose these two to send first for a reason. And that is because the best picture that we have is not quick to be seen, nor is it something that your wildest imagination would think to look for in a picture. Believe me, I know how that sounds, and thats why we have been having a hard time getting this picture out there.

So here it goes:) The best picture that we have is of a spiritual battle taking place, in that the right hand of God is grasping the enemy by the teeth. And that event occurring is biblically scriptural. All of the pictures that we have, we feel that they are a gift from God to show the world something to see with their eyes, so that they might believe in Him.

LIFTING SPIRITS

# THE HOUSE ON POULTNEY ROAD

**A True Ghost Story**

# BY

## STEPHANIE BODDY

### Chapter One

The same as most other years, the house on Poultney Road was up for sale. I grabbed the opportunity to view the house I'd heard so much about. I was desperate to be able to sift reality from the fictional image I'd created in my mind. Not wanting to go alone, and with my parents being away, I talked my disbelieving boyfriend, Elliott, into coming with me. We'd been together two years and, although we are best friends and bear no secrets, the house on Poultney Road was not something we had discussed in any great depth. The house is only thirty minutes from where I lived with my parents and the ride there was smooth. The weather was particularly warm for June and the fact that our motorway journey was surrounded by blue skies and green fields, made me feel slightly less anxious.

"I don't want to go in." Elliott said, mocking me; his piercing brown eyes absorbing my reaction.

Elliott is a sceptic. He has little faith in God and even less in the afterlife. I've wasted no time in telling him about my family's history, about what had taken over their lives for so many years. Not that he would disbelieve me or my family but I know he would find it hard to accept what they had been a part of.

"You can wait in the car if you really want to but it's going to be hard enough trying to convince the current owners that such a young couple has £450k to spend on a house let alone a single woman," I replied sternly. My expression softening, I continued, "please, I need you to support me with this."

I watched as a smile appeared on Elliott's' face. "Of course I'm coming in with you, can't wait to meet some ghosts!"

When we arrived, we parked in a space directly outside the house. I sat for a moment and looked up at the very grand but tired-looking building. The bricks were now discoloured, far from the blood red colour they had once been, and I could see that they were crumbling around the edges. I tried to envision beyond the exterior, the tatty blinds and grubby seals, and worked hard to imagine number 106 Poultney Road as my family had almost a century ago. The display of crumbling bricks and markedly worn woodwork in front of me, was once a charming, inviting home. As hard as I fought with the image in front of me, I was unable to do it; this house could never be inviting. Although it appeared nothing out of the ordinary and quite similar to the houses which surrounded it, number 106 stood alone.

The second floor had two large windows at the front of the house, which was north facing, and I could imagine it being very dark and dismal inside, so the more windows meant maximum light getting in. There was one small, square window which sat above the front door, and a larger window which replicated the one beneath it. A small window sat on the third floor, and looked as though it was the gateway to an attic or converted loft space. It looked quite dark and not very inviting. I would be giving that floor a miss. More than a century old, this house, Florence Villa, was erected in honour of Colonel Pulteney Henry Murray in 1882. A captain during the Egyptian War, the house should stand tall and represent a great man who fought for our country. It seems that, ironically, although the house was built as a mark of respect to a man who served during the war, and has withstood two world wars since then, it now has to face a continuous battle of its own. I suppose that when it was erected all those years ago, never did anyone imagine that such devastation and horror would be wrecked.

We made our way up the front steps and stood in front of the rather underwhelming, crimson-coloured front door. To the right of it was a large, rectangular window which hid thick, cigarette-tarnished net behind it.

"I don't want to go in. What happens if a ghost jumps out and scares me," Elliott mocked.

"Shut up and keep comments like that to yourself, or at least keep them quiet until we leave." I answered, unimpressed by his humour.

I think spirits and the afterlife have been so commercialised over the years that society has come to the conclusion that because it doesn't see the dead walking down the street or have spirits asking for help, that those who do experience any paranormal activity, or mediums as some people like to refer to them, are regarded as fakes.

Elliott, as I previously said, does not believe in the paranormal nor understand those who do.

We knocked on the door and waited to be greeted. I'm not sure how I felt. A combination of anxiety, fear, apprehension? I felt like I had already grown accustomed to the inside of the house because of the many stories I had been told growing up. Although I had never been inside, I felt like this house was as much part of my childhood as was my family's. It was a strange feeling when, in fact, I had no idea what was beyond the grand, red front door.

"Come in. Come in." Mrs Robinson was a well-spoken woman, perhaps recently reaching her fortieth birthday. Much taller than me, with dirty blond locks, she extended her wafer-like hand to greet me. "Have you come far?"

I could smell an underlying stench of cigarettes on her breath which usually wouldn't concern me quite as much as it did that summer evening. It almost made me retch.

"No, not really," I replied, continuing, "Have you had much interest in the property? How long has it been on the market?"

Besides her bad breath, I noticed that Mrs Robinson paused before she replied, "Since March; just two months. We've had a few people view the house but the train station at the back seems to put most of them off. I've recently asked for the ad to be more specific about the location of the property so that people come prepared. Did you see that the house was next to the station?" she asked.

"Yes," I replied, "I saw it in the description."

Already aware of the location of this property, I've always thought that this contributes to the house being even more susceptible to 'passing traffic'. Thousands of commuters fleet past every day, the house can sense life and thrives on its energy.

It was hard to believe that I was standing where it all started, so many years ago. A building which nurtured and matured several generations of my family; number 106 Poultney Road wasn't your typical haunted house. It wasn't isolated or miles from society but instead situated in a busy street next to a hectic train station used every day, every minute by commuters. As I stepped inside, it wasn't what I expected; in fact, I was disappointed. It was an anti-climax. For so many years I'd created an image in my mind of how this house should look, it's layout, decor, lighting; everything pictured perfectly in my mind to match the many stories I'd collected. Instead it felt like a grand building of emptiness.

I was immediately aware of how dark it was and how much bigger it was than what I'd expected from the online directory or even from standing outside. To my right was the front room, into which we were led.

"This is the TV room. Excuse my son, he's back from university and seems to have taken over the house."

I looked about the room. Everything appeared to be normal of that of a house more than a hundred years old. It had traditional high ceilings and a gorgeous stone fireplace which I presumed was an original feature. Her son was laid out on the brown leather sofa with his eyes glued to the television. He looked about sixteen with greasy black hair, and oily skin to match. I found it hard to believe he was old enough to be at university but it was none of my business, so didn't utter a comment. He grunted something under his breath which I guessed was some kind of greeting but I wasn't sure so didn't reply.

"So how long have you lived here?" I enquired whilst returning myself to the tour.

"Almost five years," she replied, slightly hesitant, "on and off. My husband and I own a house in Switzerland and spend most of our time there. In fact, we have tried to sell this house on several occasions but I think because of the current climate, people are choosing cheaper locations away from the city or renovating what they already own." I nodded as though I agreed with her but I knew that the recession wasn't the problem or the reason why the house was always up for sale. Although I joined in with her small talk, I never lost sight of my purpose. What I found particularly strange was the lack of atmosphere the house had. Although I was not unaccompanied and there were, with limits, furnishings around me, I felt alone.

**To carry on reading you can buy the full book here:**
http://www.amazon.co.uk/House-Poultney-Road-Stephanie-Boddy/dp/0992809223/ref=sr_1_1?ie=UTF8&qid=1410138043&sr=8-1&keywords=the+house+on+poultney+road

# The Devils Toy Box
## Considered more dangerous then the OUJIA BOARD

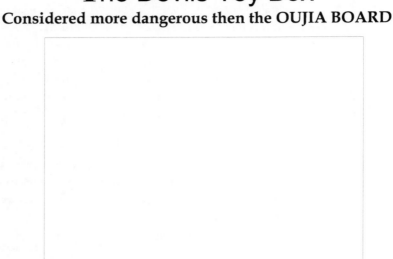

http://shop.paranormalinvestigationsequipment.com/products/the-devils-toy-box

### What is this device I hear you say?

6 mirrors all identical size, all facing each other forming a cube.. with the mirrors facing inwards

Attached with a special microphone which picks up vibrations and sound.

The idea behind this device is an interesting one to say the least!!,  this device is believed to bring fourth paranormal activity. An Energy loop that is perpetuated by the six mirrors, which can be recorded.

### More about this device

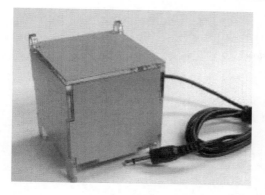

Mirrors are believed within the paranormal community to be doorways and portals to other dimensions, In fact a lot of todays pictures are captured in mirrors and windows,

With 2 mirrors facing each other, you will notice an infant image, a Mirror within a mirror, which goes on endlessly, until you can no longer see any more, which doesn't mean it ends there... Now adding more mirrors is going to create more reflections and more Infinite images and double the energy within the cube.

His idea behind it, is that mirrors can work as a window to bring fourth paranormal activity. An Energy loop that is perpetuated by the six mirrors making up the cube.
http://www.abovetopsecret.com

It is believed that when we combine the mirrors, it is like adding a signal booster to the reception on a different wavelength http://www.pandoricahelp.com

Its believed that Wiccan's of the past supposedly used the box to trap and transfer negative energies, and it wasn't until 2012 when someone decided to look more into this field, and conduct research. The results he found was "out of this world" "phenomenal" and the longer you leave the box the more energy you will get coming thought the mic.

**THE TEST**

*LEE STEER FROM PARANORMAL MAGAZINE AND PROJECT-REVEAL DECIDED TO PUT THE DEVICE TO THE TEST.*

Using an Olympus VN3200

Now there is a number of experiments I would like to try with this device.

- Plugging an GUITAR AMP into the box, and listing to LIVE audio, where you can play with the gain and noise.
- Putting trigger objects within the box, which could be connected to a person or house.
- Putting a light source into the box
- Put a camera into the box
- use a franks box on top of the box

There will be more experiments I can think of but my first one, was a standard recording session.

I wasn't expecting to get any sounds but after 15 mins, I started to hear a slight hissing.. 5 mins later we started to get some scratching sounds..

"there was nothing in the box"

so as a sceptic I cannot explain what was causing the scratching and growls, this device manages to block out around 75% of human sound. due to the construction of the mirror and the microphone inside.

overall this device has left me scratching my head..
MORE EXPERIMENTS TO COME

people say this device captures spirits, its safe to say I
let them out…

Wait… maybe that's a bad thing!!!!

**I urge all paranormal researchers an paranormal
investigators to look more into this!!**

**Visit**

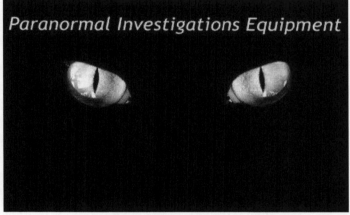

http://www.paranormalinvestigationsequipment.com

# ATDD Teddy
## ©HauntedSolutions.Com

The new ATTD Teddy by haunted solutions Is the first of its kind and
has been designed to communicate with spirit children or spirits by
using temperature. Craig & Amira Company Directors At Haunted
Solutions Ltd Based In Paisley, Scotland. Are The Original Designers
Behind The EMF Teddy That Featured On (Ghost Hunters Orphans of
Gettysburg Season 9 Episode 17 In 2014. Since then the EMF Teddy
has been copied worldwide. Craig & Amira from Haunted Solutions
say At haunted solutions we knew it would be copied to many degrees
within the paranormal and ghost hunting industry. But at Haunted
Solutions we build things with a theory behind it and our theory was
proved to us. And Continues to be backed up by the Original EMF
Teddies that are used and are going into the field. When we launched
the EMF Teddy Back 2012, We started work on the ATDD not long
after. At HauntedSolutions.com We work close with the guys at D.A.S
And as investigators ourselves we have had a lot of great evidence
with D.A.S ATDD, And Without going into to much detail, we started
building the ATDD Teddy.
(The New ATDD Teddy Contains A Genuine ATDD, The
Same ATDD Located In Your Mel-Rem-ATDD Meters)

The ATDD Teddy is designed specifically to monitor and detect a +5 deg. / -5 deg. ambient temperature (deviation) change that occurs within an environment. When a temperature shift does occur, the device will react quickly and produce a unique, one octave "step" tone for each individual degree change. Incremental "+" changes have a higher pitch while descending "-" temperature drops have a lower pitch. This allows the paranormal investigator to "hear" and validate any temperature change around the device from up to 50' away (line of sight).

This device can also help investigators become more efficient and thorough by helping to monitor remote unattended areas throughout a house or building during an investigation and help direct attention to an area that may have paranormal activity. In addition, the ATDD device utilizes RED LEDs for a "+" temperature change and BLUE LEDs for a "-" change.

A single multi-purpose push button is used to "Tare" the circuit and mute the sound in any of the three configurations.

# Submit your content now for issue 5

**Issue 5 release date is 1$^{st}$ January 2015.**

**You can submit anything paranormal related like:**

ghost story's
Pictures
Equipment reviews "you must not be selling it"
How to's
Interviews
or Ask a Question for us to answer in issue 5
visit

**Do all of the above by contacting us at the below url**
http://paranormal-magazine.com/contact-us/

**TO SELL**
**Advertise in this book for as little as £10.00 Pounds,**
Since this book will remain for sale, your ad you be in the book for its
lifetime, bought by 1000s of paranormal enthusiasts, each month in the
form of: Paperback & kindle worldwide

**Great for advertising Ghost Hunts, Equipment, Discount codes,
Etc.**

*Half a page £10.00*
*Full-page £20.00*

*2 pages £30.00*

**Email** asteer8@aol.com

**Ghost Hunts**

### Other Ghost hunts:
Swadlincote - Old Gresley Hall £25.00 per person 27/09/2014
Nottingham - Strelley Hall £30.00 per person 11/10/2014
Yorkshire - Saltmarshe Hall £30.00 per person 18/10/2014
The Old House - Leicestershire £35.00 per person 01/11/2014
Warwick - St Johns Museum £39.00 per person 08/11/2014
For more visit http://ukghosthunts.com

# Thank you
# for reading issue 4

Printed in Great Britain
by Amazon.co.uk, Ltd.,
Marston Gate.